LIGHTNING
BOLT
BOOKS

Magic Tricks with Props

Elsie Olson

Lerner Publications • Minneapolis

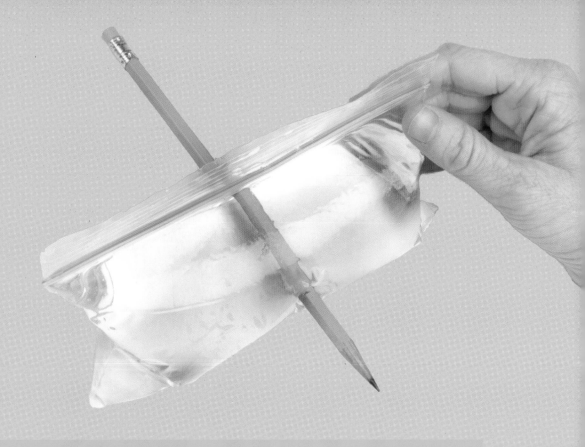

Lerner Publications Company
A division of Lerner Publishing Group, Inc.
241 First Avenue North
Minneapolis, MN 55401 USA

For reading levels and more information, look up this title at www.lernerbooks.com.

Library of Congress Cataloging-in-Publication Data

Names: Olson, Elsie, 1986- author.
Title: Magic tricks with props / by Elsie Olson.
Description: Minneapolis : Lerner Publications, 2019. | Series: Lightning bolt books. magic tricks | Includes bibliographical references and index. | Audience: Age 6-9. | Audience: K to Grade 3
Identifiers: LCCN 2018011216 (print) | LCCN 2018013579 (ebook) | ISBN 9781541543409 (eb pdf) | ISBN 9781541538955 (lb : alk. paper)
Subjects: LCSH: Magic tricks—Juvenile literature. | Magic tricks—Equipment and supplies—Juvenile literature.
Classification: LCC GV1548 (ebook) | LCC GV1548 .O484 2019 (print) | DDC 793.8—dc23

LC record available at https://lccn.loc.gov/2018011216

Manufactured in the United States of America
1-45078-35905-6/22/2018

Table of Contents

Getting Started

Have you ever watched a magician perform? There is a secret behind every trick. Magicians perform tricks using props. With practice, you can do prop tricks too!

Prop Trick Tips

- **Get permission.** Ask an adult if it's OK to perform these prop tricks. Make sure you are allowed to use the materials. And get help when using scissors or other sharp objects.

- **Tell a story!** Make up a story to tell while doing each trick. This will make the trick more fun for your audience.

- **Add more props.**

Adding props such as a magic wand can help make tricks your own.

- **Practice!** It can take a long time to perfect a trick. Practice in front of a mirror until you are ready to perform.

Not So Tricky

Magic Pencil Push

Amaze your audience with an unlikely leak-proof bag.

What you need:

- Zipper-close plastic bag
- Water
- Sharpened pencil

Getting ready:

Fill the plastic bag with water and seal it.

The trick:

1. Show your audience the bag of water. Let them pass it around to prove that it is an ordinary bag.

2. Show the audience the pencil.

3. Explain that you are going to enchant the water to stay in the bag. Use your pencil as a magic wand.

4. Carefully push the pencil through both sides of the bag. Even with two holes in the bag, the water does not leak!

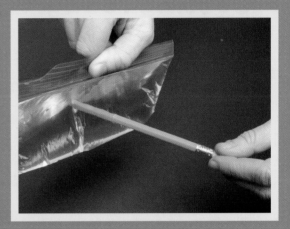

Secret Sliced Banana

Feed your entire audience with this clever banana trick.

What you need:

- Banana
- Clean straight pin

Getting ready:

1. Use the pin to cut the unpeeled banana into slices. To cut a slice, carefully push the pin through the peel and into the banana. But don't push the pin out the other side of the peel! Wiggle the pin from side to side to cut the banana.

2. Repeat step 1 as you move in a line down the length of the banana.

Straight pins are sharp! Be careful when getting this project ready.

The trick:

1. Show your audience that you are holding an ordinary banana. Keep the side with the pin holes facing away from the audience.

2. Tell your audience that you have only one banana and no knife. You'd like to give a piece of the banana to everyone. Say you are going to slice the banana with your mind.

3. Look at the banana and pretend to concentrate. You could even give the banana a command, like "Slice!"

4. Peel the banana and offer the slices to your amazed audience.

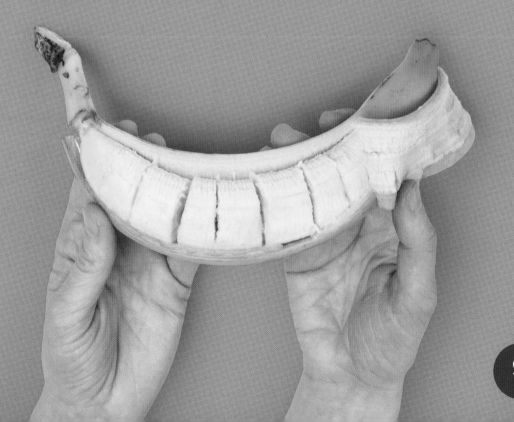

A Little Tricky

Magic Rising Ring

Mystify your audience when you command a ring to rise using only your voice!

What you need:

- Rubber band
- Ring
- Scissors

Getting ready:

1. Carefully cut the rubber band so it is a long piece with two ends.

2. Pinch the rubber band between your right thumb and pointer finger several inches from one end. Hide the rest of that end in your right hand.

It should look to your audience as if you are pinching the end of the rubber band.

The trick:

1. Thread the free end of the rubber band through the ring.

2. Pinch the free end of the rubber band between your left thumb and pointer finger.

3. Pull the rubber band tight with your left hand slightly higher than the right. Let the ring fall toward your right hand.

4. Say, "Rise!" Keeping your hands in the exact same position, gently loosen the grip of your right thumb and pointer finger. This will slowly release the extra rubber band in your right hand. As you do so, the ring will appear to rise!

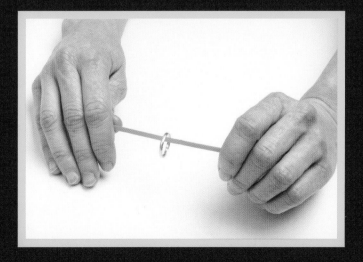

Paper Clip Hop

Wow your friends when two paper clips
magically hop together.

What you need:

- Dollar bill
- 2 paper clips

The trick:

1. Fold the bill into a Z shape, so it is divided into
    three layers.

2. Slide one paper clip onto the front edge of the
    bill so it connects the top two layers of the bill.
    The short part of the clip should face up.

3. Slide the second paper clip onto the front edge of the bill so it connects the bottom two layers of the bill. Be sure it is to the right of the first clip when you are looking at it. The short part of the clip should face down.

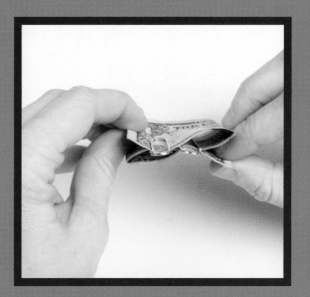

4. Gently tug on the two short ends of the bill to straighten it out. When you do so, the paper clips will hop off the bill and link together!

Double Your Money!

Dazzle your fans when you turn one coin into two coins!

What you need:

- 2 pennies

Getting ready:

1. Squeeze one penny, face up, between your thumb and pointer finger.

2. Place the second penny, face out, between your thumb and pointer finger. The first penny should be perpendicular to the second penny.

Turn your back to the audience while you set up your coins or get ready in a separate room.

The trick:

1. Show the audience the face-out penny. Angle your hand so they cannot see the face-up penny. Tell them you are going to double your money.

2. Cup your empty hand over the penny hand. Bring both pennies into the palm of the penny hand.

3. Say a magic word and shake the pennies. The audience will hear that there are now two coins!

4. Open your hand to reveal the two pennies.

Terrifically Tricky

Magic Rabbit Tube

Shock your audience when you pull a paper rabbit out of an empty tube!

What you need:

- Small paper rabbit, no bigger than a playing card. You can make this yourself!
- 2 sheets of paper
- Clear tape
- Scissors

Getting ready:

1. Roll one sheet of paper the long way to make a tube. Tape it in place.

2. Roll the second sheet of paper the long way to make a cone. The large end of the cone should be the same size as the opening of the tube. Tape it in place.

3. Slide the cone into the tube. Trim off any cone edges that stick out. You now have a hiding place between the small end of the cone and the tube!

4. Put the rabbit in the hiding place. You may want to tape it so it doesn't fall out during the trick.

The trick:

1. Show your audience the tube opening. Make sure the cone's large end is facing them.

2. Explain that with your magical powers, you are going to pull a rabbit out of the tube.

3. Wave your hand over the tube and say, "Abracadabra."

4. Pull the rabbit out of the hiding place and show it to your audience!

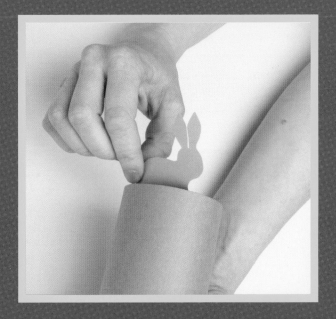

Floating Friends

Impress your audience when a photo mysteriously floats through the air.

What you need:

- Photo of your friends
- Plastic drinking straw
- 12-inch (30 cm) piece of clear fishing line
- Tape

Getting ready:

1. Cut two short pieces off the straw. Tape them next to each other on the back of the photo. The holes of the straws should face left and right.

2. Thread the fishing line through the straws. Tie a loop at one end of the line.

3. Tape the other end of the line to the back of the photo, making another loop.

4. Put one thumb through the tied loop. Slip the other thumb through the other loop.

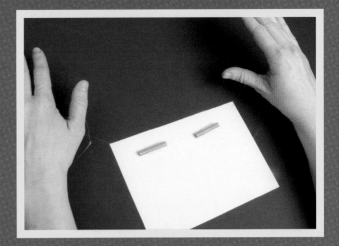

5. Slide the photo on the string toward the tied loop.

The trick:

1. Spread open your hands so your palms face the audience. The photo will appear to float between your hands.

2. Slowly and gently move the hand with the tied loop away from your other hand. The photo will seem to move on its own!

Prop Trick Tidbits

- One of the most well-known prop tricks is pulling a live rabbit out of a top hat. The rabbit is hidden in a secret compartment or bag beneath the hat. These days, magicians rarely perform this trick because it is scary for the animal.

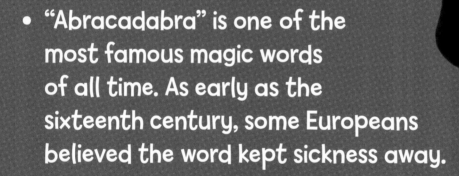

- "Abracadabra" is one of the most famous magic words of all time. As early as the sixteenth century, some Europeans believed the word kept sickness away.

- The first book about magic tricks was published in 1584. It was called *The Discoverie of Witchcraft*, by Englishman Reginald Scot.

Meet a Magician!

David Copperfield

David Copperfield is one of the most famous magicians of all time. He was born David Kotkin in Metuchen, New Jersey, in 1956. When he was just 12 years old, he became the youngest member of the Society of American Magicians. Some of Copperfield's best-known tricks involve very famous and very large props. He once made the Statue of Liberty disappear in front of a live audience. In another trick, he seemed to walk through the Great Wall of China!

Glossary

compartment: a separate closed space used to hold something

concentrate: to direct one's attention or energy toward something

enchant: to charm or put under a spell

magician: a person who performs magic tricks

mystify: to confuse or puzzle

perpendicular: meeting at a right angle, like the lines in the letter T

prop: an object a performer uses to create a certain effect

Further Reading

Funology — Object Tricks
http://www.funology.com/category/magic-tricks
/object-tricks/

Higginson, Sheila Sweeny. *Pulling Back the Curtain on Magic*. New York: Simon Spotlight, 2015.

Jay, Joshua. *Big Magic for Little Hands*. New York: Workman Pub., 2014.

Kelly, Kristen. *Abracadabra! Fun Magic Tricks for Kids.* New York: Sky Pony Press, 2016.

Kidspot — Make a Trick Magic Wand
http://www.kidspot.com.au/things-to-do/activity
-articles/make-a-trick-magic-wand/news-story/cf
c37daa96776601a8256031a4647397?ref=collecti
on_view,magic-tricks

Magic Tricks for Kids — Rope Trick
http://magictricksforkids.org/rope-trick/

Index

Photo Acknowledgments

The images in this book are used with the permission of: © Mighty Media, Inc., pp. 2, 6, 7 (top), 7 (bottom), 8, 9, 10, 11 (top), 11 (bottom), 12, 13 (top), 13 (bottom), 14, 15 (top), 15 (bottom), 17 (top), 17 (bottom), 18, 19 (top), 19 (bottom); © Shutterstock, pp. 4, 20, 21; © iStockphoto, p. 5.

Front cover: © 123RF (top middle); © Shutterstock (left, bottom middle, right).

Main body text set in Billy Infant.